Stop Wasting Time and Burning Money

How to Crush Procrastination & Live the Life of Your Dreams

Ryan J. Rhoades & Lany Sullivan

Stop Wasting Time and Burning Money

How to Crush Procrastination & Live the Life of Your Dreams

Ryan J. Rhoades & Lany Sullivan

ISBN 978-1500780234

This is a Leanpub book. Leanpub empowers authors and publishers with the Lean Publishing process. Lean Publishing is the act of publishing an in-progress ebook using lightweight tools and many iterations to get reader feedback, pivot until you have the right book and build traction once you do.

Tweet This Book!

Please help Ryan J. Rhoades & Lany Sullivan by spreading the word about this book on Twitter!

The suggested tweet for this book is:

Are you ready to #StopWastingTime & Burning Money? Get a FREE #productivity workbook here: www.StopWastingTime.Today

The suggested hashtag for this book is #StopWastingTime.

Find out what other people are saying about the book by clicking on this link to search for this hashtag on Twitter:

https://twitter.com/search?q=#StopWastingTime

This book is dedicated to all those who have chosen to take the road less traveled and know in their heart that it has made all the difference.

(Yeah, that's also a shout out to Robert Frost.)

Contents

CONTENTS

Before You Get Started...

We wrote this book to help you along the journey of life and business.

As you read, you will find that we provide resources, wisdom, and exercises that you will benefit from most if you follow along with the complimentary workbook that we have created.

The workbook can be used as a standalone product and you are free to share the download link with your social networks, families and friends.

Please make sure to download and print out the workbook before reading further.

We believe you will find that they work very well together!

Enjoy!

Download the workbook for FREE @ www.StopWastingTime.Today

Endorsements

"This book is an easy read with a powerful message. You feel like the authors are reading your mind as they call out bad habits so many of us have and show you how to stop wasting time and anchor yourself on results."

— Danielle Miller

"This book was a much needed kick in the right direction for me! Full of practical steps to help you establish what's REALLY important in your life, and then, crucially - the steps to help you FOLLOW THROUGH.

*So many books of this nature don't really offer any **practical** help - this one really delivers!*

I also downloaded the free workbook and printed out the worksheets - this is probably the best way to get the full benefit of this brilliant little book.

Highly recommended!"

— Rebecca Clayton

"I'm a procrastinator, guilty as charged. I've tried the time management books, they try to create systems for you that are either going to work or not, and most of the time, for me, they don't. By contrast, Stop Wasting Time, and the companion worksheets, are completely different. Lany and Ryan took an inner approach at identifying why we waste time, and it clicked.

— Stephan Hovnanian

"Most of us are guilty, from time to time, of becoming extremely "busy" but not actually being "productive." My level of actual productivity is something that I feel the need to periodically measure, and that analysis can often require adjustments (be they large or small) to get myself back on track and back to the level I wish to be operating at.

Already using several of the same tech tools that Ryan and Lany share about in their book, I definitely had interest in diving in deeper, to see what other ideas they might offer. It proved well worth the read. In addition to walking you through some goal setting, the book contains valuable tips on sticking to the plan you create and methods of managing time more successfully. I personally need to make sure to occasionally revisit their "Income Producing Activities" section, because using that lens to view my task list through is something I often forget to do.

— Mark Powers

"Anyone who knows me knows that I read a lot and I also am a "planning person". I have plan for everything. While that can be annoying to family members, it works for me. Let me tell you what Lany Sullivan and Ryan J. Rhoades have accomplished with their book.

They helped me change the way that I was thinking about my future. I usually have a firm grasp on my goals but as I worked through the workbook provided and started digging deeper I found out I had forgotten about what I really wanted. I had not really thought about what I wanted my future to look like & I had not envisioned my goals.

From the bottom of my heart, thanks to both of you. I will send you a postcard from my trip to Paris. Great work, guys!"

— L. Williams

Preface to the Second Edition

"Our busyness is a choice."

-Ryan J. Rhoades

If there is one phrase I needed to remind myself of as I approached getting ready to publish the second edition/paperback version of this book, it is this one.

Written over a year ago, it is even something that you will see highlighted multiple times throughout what you're about to read.

But it's so easy to get busy, right?

Look, I get it!

For example, right now, on top of trying to get this book published, we also are working on designing and publishing books for our clients.

And creating their logos. And their marketing materials. And their social media presence.

And launch our clothing line.

And get caught up on paperwork.

And launch a new version of our online store (that's at store.reformationdesigns.com, by the way)

And prep and launch a whole new line of inspirational high quality art prints and posters.

And figure out how to hire help.

And figure out how to design several logos for industries I've never worked in before.

And finish building several client websites.

And launch StartupSalem.com.

And oh yeah.

Live an active, fulfilling life and start a family and enjoy the time that I have with them on this planet.

You know, the important thing. The thing that we do all of the crazy things for.

The big important thing that somehow manages to get lost in the midst of all the things we do to try and keep the big important thing the big important thing.

It has almost been a year since we released the first e-book version of what you now hold in your hands.

The work involved in creating this book is more than I ever thought it would be.

It was written on the backs of napkins, on my phone in bathroom stalls, in the middle of the night, on laptops, on tablets, edited, re-edited, the cover was redesigned...TWICE...and across various note taking platforms (all of which we mention in the book).

We thought we were ready to go with the paperback and ran into a year's worth of obstacles.

But it's here.

And the response so far has been fantastic.

I hear stories from all over the world of people that have simply followed the game plan we lay out in this book that are seeing debts paid off, financial freedom, and more time and energy spent with loved ones doing the big important things instead of the crazy-making busy things.

And I'm the first to admit - this year has been one of the craziest yet. My wife and I had to move suddenly after finally getting settled into a new apartment because the foundation had black mold in it. Right under where our bed was.

We had just unpacked one of the last boxes and felt like we could relax. A few days later, it rained like crazy and we discovered the problem.

We were out in 24 hours.

I'm still wrangling with the property owners trying to get them to pay to replace our bed and other things that were ruined.

Then, after I received the proof copy of this book in the mail to review, edit, proofread and all of that jazz, one of our pets had to visit the veterinary ER and it turned into a $2,000+ ordeal over the course of the next two months. This was during the week of Thanksgiving.

We had Chinese food.

When that finally started to settle, a few days before Christmas I found out that my father (way out on the east coast) was in the hospital. That lasted through Christmas.

The stress of knowing a loved one was in the hospital but due to other circumstances we weren't able to be there - well, let's just say we ate Chinese food on Christmas day, too.

I'm not sharing all of this to give you a huge sob story.

I share it to let you know, as we do elsewhere throughout the book, that *I am just like you.* I have life issues pop up that are unexpected, frustrating, depressing, scary, crazy, rage-inducing...and yes there are even fun things that happen too!

Yet despite all of it - at the end of the day - everything we do and everything we believe is a choice.

We may not be able to control what happens *to* us, but we can train ourselves to think in a way where we are empowered to make healthier choices in *response* to what happens to us.

That has always been one of my goals with my writing: to share what I have learned through trial and error (lots of error) in an attempt to save the reader from making the same mistakes I did.

Doing your own thing is not easy.

It is one of the most challenging, frustrating, and life-altering things you could possibly ever decide to do.

I had no idea when my wife and I decided to start our first business that it would basically be like choosing to have our first child.

The amount of attention, time, money, and energy involved in keeping the thing alive are certainly comparable!

But it also is one of the most rewarding, beneficial, educational, and inspiring things you could possibly ever decide to do.

It has taken a long time - much longer than I thought it would - to get to a point where we know beyond the shadow of a doubt that there's no turning back to the 9-5 world that we left behind 7 years ago.

There certainly are still times that we consider it - but when we weigh the freedoms that we have to work when we want, with who we want, how we want, and where we want against a stationary life taking orders all day every day?

There's no contest.

We are in this for the long haul. And that *choice* has made all the difference when we are in the trenches and things are tough.

That *choice* is like a compass that keeps us headed in the right direction even when we feel like we don't know where we're going.

If you are considering setting out on your own journey away from the 9-5, consider the cost before doing so.

Make sure you know why you're doing it. There are statistics that say that 9 out of 10 startups fail. My wife and I decided a long time ago that we would not be like that 90%.

Read that again:

We *decided* that we would not be like that 90%.

Because when the rough days come, and they will, it is the choices you make and the mindsets you have when you first start out that will determine what you do when it seems like the world is falling down around you.

We had to learn how to champion one another when things got difficult. We had to learn how to hang up inspirational posters (that we designed) all over our home so that no matter where we look, every wall and every room reminds us of where we're going and why.

We don't have a committee or a superior whose job it is to make sure that we stay productive, or know how to market our services, or what products to focus on building first, or how to balance a budget, or where to look for new clients, or how to self-publish a book, or how to build websites, or the art of branding, or how to draw a crowd and lead a tribe of entrepreneurs and aspiring entrepreneurs through the minefield of life and business.

We had to learn how to do it on our own.

We had to turn off the TV and focus on creating.

We had to switch off Netflix and get writing.

And we *definitely* had to get the hell off of social media and stop the mindless scrolling and looking for something better to fall out of the sky.

We realized a long time ago that the only people who were going to really work on building the life that *we* wanted to live, was us.

Nobody was going to make us learn the art of setting healthy boundaries for ourselves and others, or how to stop feeling too busy to do the things that we really cared about deep down.

We had to make those decisions on our own.

We wanted something more than what the status quo was promising.

So we went out and got it. And what you now see before you is one of the results of that decision.

At the end of the day, **it all started with a choice.**

Lany and I published the e-book version of this book back in November of 2014. It has taken almost two years to get to a point where we were ready to turn what you're reading into a "real book".

In that time, there were just as many (if not more) ups and downs as the years prior.

There were emergencies that came up. There were projects that pushed the publish date on this book back further and further.

And yes, dear reader, we procrastinated and didn't follow through on the time tables that we had set for ourselves regarding launch dates, etc.

We do not consider ourselves to be above reproach or mistakes. Far from it. We wrote this book because we have struggled intensely with the very things we now help others with.

We want to make it clear that we do not expect you to follow the instructions we provide in this book to a T.

The last thing that we would wish is for you to feel even more burdened by your schedule than you already are after having read this.

Our goal has always and will always be to empower you to take what works for you from the resources we have provided and work it to your benefit and the benefit of your loved ones.

We do not use all of the tools that we have mentioned in this work.

We have *tried* them all - but as with anything, we found what worked for us and what didn't.

It is our wish that you would do the same - so don't beat yourself up if you haven't gotten everything done that you set out to do.

Make it a point to focus on the things you have accomplished that you set your mind to and be thankful for those successes.

They will give you the momentum to leap towards that next milestone.

One of the beneficial things that this last year has afforded us is the ability to gain valuable feedback from our readers.

A dear friend of mine from the UK let me know recently that her and her husband had paid off a debt that had been lingering for quite some time as a result of going through this book and applying the principles we mentioned.

Others have told us of their success stories as well - and each goal that was accomplished came as a direct result of intentional planning and even more intentional action.

It is a huge encouragement to us to hear that the work that we have produced has been helping the kinds of people that we set out to help: people just like you.

We live in a time where the only barriers to fulfilling the dreams that we have for our lives are self-imposed limiting beliefs.

The technology at all of our fingertips continues to expand exponentially and has made a way for anyone to do just about anything they put their minds to.

You can be a self-published author.

We are.

You can be self-employed.

We are.

You can escape the 9-5 and live your life on purpose and accomplish goals that *you* set for yourself.

We did.

You can work with some of the most influential and amazing people on the planet.

We have.

So many people are waiting for permission to get started on building their dreams.

You have it. If you're looking for a sign, let this be it.

You can achieve everything you put your mind to. This isn't some hyped-up self-help mumbo jumbo. It's true.

We never have said it would be easy. We simply said it was possible.

If you're reading this book in the first place, there are certain assumptions that we make about the type of person that you are.

People who want to tow the party line and fit in with the status quo don't buy books like this.

Or maybe you're just tired of working the same job with the same responsibilities and putting up with the petty politics of the same people on a power trip.

Know this: **you are not alone**.

The decision to continue when everyone else is ready to throw in the towel is what separates those who are truly "successful" from those who are not.

That next call you make could land you a multi-million dollar deal.

That next sentence that you write could save someone's life who was considering ending theirs.

That simple word of advice might save your employer thousands of dollars and net you a great promotion.

Don't be afraid to speak up and share what you know to be true. Don't be afraid to pursue the dreams that have long been dormant in your mind.

And more than that, don't be afraid to pick up those things that you have left unfinished and start working at them when you have more experience and wisdom under your belt.

You wouldn't be reading this if we hadn't done so.

As the old adage says, the journey of a thousand miles begins with the first step.

So above all else, enjoy the journey ahead of you. Give yourself the grace to take your time.

One of the hardest things to do when you are in the pursuit of something you love is to be okay with where you are instead of stressing out about where you aren't.

The rewards of this pursuit combined with the patience required to do anything that is "outside the box" far outweigh the costs.

Thanks for sharing this journey with us. We wish you well in your travels.

-Ryan J. Rhoades - Salem, OR - June 2016

Introduction by Ryan J. Rhoades

As much as I like getting stuff done, at the end of the day **if something isn't fun, I don't like to do it and often have a heck of a time getting started just like you do**.

Over the years, I have found that there are methods and techniques for being productive that are actually quite fun once you get the hang of them.

So why write another book about time management/productivity/etc.?

Well, for one, after spending years reading books on running a business, leadership, and things of that sort, I kept finding myself increasingly frustrated at how seriously everyone seemed to take themselves.

It felt like there was this prevailing mentality when writing or talking about anything even remotely *business-y* or "self-help" related, that it has to be insanely serious.

Most of the books I came across had a huge focus on facts, figures, data, and technique as opposed to helping people change the way they think about the way they're going about their everyday lives.

More than that, I found that there were a lot of books where the "successful" authors talked extensively of the amazing successes that they've had, but very rarely actually shared the HOW of how they got there.

Lany and I decided to put together this book in an effort to show you that you really can be more productive, stop wasting your time doing frivolous things that don't make you happy, and even make money in the process...

But more than that, we wanted to do this our way.

We wanted to present you with material that was practical, fun, occasionally humorous, and create something that would become a resource you would be happy to share with your friends and family as you all work together building the life that you want.

We didn't go through any official publishers to create what you're now reading. We didn't hire ghost writers to write our book for us.

We didn't pay someone to compile things we've said or done into a manuscript and then take all the credit for writing the book.

We worked together remotely from different states using various new technologies (which we will discuss later in the book) in order to create what you now have in front of you.

We live in an age when the number of gatekeepers in the publishing world and obstacles to releasing your own products and services continues to drop to zero.

The opportunities that are available to you this very moment are ones that have only become an option within the last several years because of advances in technology and innovators around the world.

There's something almost magical about holding something

that you've created...whether that's a book, a piece of art-work, a screenplay, or wearing a t-shirt that you've designed yourself.

It's an addictive feeling. For me, there's nothing like it in the world. But it also takes work - *a lot of it* - to be able to stay **consistent** with the creative process...that is, working on something until it's finished.

Seeing a project through to the end of the creative process has historically been one of my biggest struggles. The irony of writing a book about beating procrastination that ultimately took a couple of years to finally publish is not lost upon me.

For example, when writing that last sentence, I literally got up right after writing it and walked away distracting myself because doing this stuff can be really, really **hard**.

But at the end of the day - it is in knowing the things that I share with the world are helping people that keeps me going. It can be a scary thing to put something new out into the world...especially a world full of people who can become experts at criticizing instead of putting in the work it takes to create.

For both Lany and I, this will be our first official book. I have manuscripts all over the place: half-written, partially written, needing to be edited, etc...but have never pulled the trigger on actually releasing an official book until now.

Going the co-author route certainly helps because you can keep each other accountable to get things done on time.

I share all this to let you know that I am just like you.

It is not easy to stay productive in a culture that is constantly vying for your attention and demanding that you drop whatever you're doing to look at some advertisement on TV, the web, or your phone.

But with the right amount of discipline, practice, resources, persistence, and patience, you really can become a much more productive person.

That's the magic formula for success: work, discipline, and grit.

It is my hope that this book helps you along at least one step further in becoming the person you've always wanted to be.

I want to champion you to achieve your goals and fulfill your dreams. What you see before you is one of my fulfilled dreams that has taken years to accomplish.

If there is one thing that I really want readers of this book to know when they are finished it is what I'm learning even as I write these words:

Be patient with yourself. The creative process is just that: a process.

I hope you enjoy our first book.

— Ryan J. Rhoades / Salem, Oregon 11/12/14

Introduction by Lany Sullivan

People often tell me that I get more done in one day than most people do in a week.

I have to admit that I still have plenty of down time, but the key is I GET STUFF DONE.

I'm a GSD Girl.

Do you want to learn how to be a GSD girl or guy? I have been in practice and implementation mode for 15+ years, so I would say that I've gotten to a point where I can do this quite well.

Let me tell you a story.

When I was 19 years old, I was working for a finance company and I had just been promoted from Sales Assistant (which was a glorified title for receptionist or admin assistant at the time).

It was my first-ever office job.

I was going to school 30 hours a week and working at this awesome job 30+ hours a week.

You see, I was working in an office that was only open during banking hours and I was going to school during the day. I was only supposed to work 24 hours a week, but **there was always more work than time.**

Can anyone relate to that?

More work to do than there is time in the day?

I was attempting to squeeze 40+ hours of work into a 24-30 hour work week, but my co-workers were all working 40 hours a week and doing just fine.

Here I was going to school full time, working full time and living like stress was an extra part-time job. It's no wonder I have gray hair at an early age. Sheesh!

My manager and I eventually started butting heads constantly. I was unorganized and ALL over the place. I was productive in one sense and closing deals, but I was also really scatter-brained which started to affect the rest of the team.

Pro-Tip: When your issues start affecting those around you it's time to realize that there is a problem and it's probably you.

Remember, I was 19 and thought I knew it all.

Don't tell me you were never a know-it-all teenager! You can't fool me!

Anyway, my manager sat me down one day with a schedule that kept me on a leash. Every minute of my day while at work was planned to the "T"!

I hated it.

I despised it!

I wanted to buck the system. I wanted to transfer to another office.

But I knew that if I wanted to keep that job, I had to make the choice to follow her schedule and reassess how I handled the things I needed to get done.

And wouldn't you know it? Her plan to help me be more productive worked great!

I'm not afraid to admit now, many years later, that it is possible to change your ingrained habits.

Thanks to those six intense months of training, I now know what I can accomplish and how to manage myself.

I use calendars to schedule my day-to-day activities and I put alarms and notifications on everything to make sure I stay on task.

I say all this to let you know that everything that we will share in this book has worked for me and I practice daily at the techniques that we will present.

Life is certainly not perfect, but when you can re-organize your priorities, consider new possibilities with an open mind and learn to make better choices, you can begin to manage your life quite easily.

I encourage you to dive in and be willing to learn. Apply the tips, tricks and tools that we share here and let us know how you become more focused and efficient!

If you honor yourself and hold yourself accountable throughout this book you will see major changes in your life and your business.

You are now well on your way to saving time and making more money, and we look forward to being part of your journey!

— Lany Sullivan, November 2014, Oregon

CHAPTER 1: How Are You?

"I'm busy."

"There are not enough hours in the day."

"I forget more things than ever these days."

"If it doesn't go into my calendar, it does not exist."

"If only I could have an extra 5 hours in my day..."

"I don't have enough time..."

Do you find yourself making these kinds of statements often?

Has the fact that you feel so busy and overwhelmed all of the time made its way into the beginning of every conversation you have?

Well, before we get started, we are going to award you with your Busy Badge!

We award this badge to people who are so busy that their current level of busy-ness is pretty much the first thing they mention when asked, *"How are you?"*

So go ahead.

Take a moment to print out the accompanying workbook if you haven't already.

You can access it from www.stopwastingtime.today.

(And yes, we know that domain name is amazing.)

At the beginning of the workbook you will find a high resolution version of the Busy Badge that you can print out and wear (not so) proudly.

Rest assured, dear reader - we understand the plight that you find yourself in.

That is why we have worked tirelessly to bring this book and workbook combo to you.

We get it.

Everyone is "busy."

So why is it that there are some people who seem to get an infinitely larger number of productive things accomplished in 24 hours than others?

We are all given the same 24 hours to do with as we will.

And before you get any further in this book, we need to be on the same page about something - and that is right here, right now, you agree to admit to yourself that you are **choosing** to do just about everything you do in a day.

Yes, that includes the job you're currently working at.

Yes, that includes the bills that you're paying.

Yes, that includes the unhealthy relationships that you continue to put up with.

At the end of the day, you are making thousands of conscious (or subconscious) choices throughout the span of 24 hours that have brought you to your current state of being.

Your choices have been influenced by a variety of factors, of course.

Things you learned in school, church, work, from your parents, family members, friends, ex-boyfriends or girlfriends, etc...

You have definitely been influenced by books that you've chosen to read, arguments that you've had, and people that have hurt you in one way or another.

The thing that you've got to settle in your mind before you will start to see real, lasting, positive changes in your life is that you may not necessarily be able to control the EVENTS that happen, but you most certainly can control your RESPONSE to those events.

Best-selling author and world-renown speaker Jack Canfield has a simple formula that he shares with his clients and audience that has dramatically changed the way we look at our lives and circumstances.

It is E + R = O

EVENT + RESPONSE = OUTCOME

You are making a choice right now as to whether or not you're going to believe what we just said.

Does this make you feel angry? Why?

Do you believe that you are the result of everything that has happened to you, or do you believe that you are more than that?

If you don't believe that you are more than that, you will always be tossed back and forth by the trials that life throws at all of us.

What we want to help you do is to learn how to respond positively to the events in your life so that you achieve the outcome and goals that you desire.

And one of the first steps to doing that is by recognizing that busyness is NOT something that happens TO you.

Busyness is something that you ALLOW to happen based solely on choices that you have made.

You choose to be too busy to do this or that.

You have made choices to do one thing and not another. You choose to sleep in late. You choose to procrastinate on those projects until the very last second.

So that stress that you may be feeling about that thing that you waited until 3 hours before the deadline to start?

That's self-inflicted.

Or that dull rage you experience when you're spending 3+ hours of every day of the week crawling by in traffic just so that you can sit in a cubicle working at a job that you hate?

So is that.

"Wait a second! I NEED to work this job because of...."

Hold on there, champ. We're just trying to get you to see that you are a powerful person that is capable of making powerful choices, and each one of those choices has consequences - some positive, and some negative.

So yes, even the stress you probably feel because you hate your job is in a way still self-inflicted because you still ultimately are **CHOOSING** to be working at that particular place that you may not be so fond of.

Remember - there are plenty of people around the world who are doing things that they love and earning a livable income doing so.

If they can do it, so can you.

Keep in mind here, folks - we're not saying that these choices are easy choices to make.

We're not saying that the road you will travel after making those choices won't be full of difficulties. It most certainly will.

We're just pointing out that ultimately, the kinds of things that you allow in your life are most often the result of choices that you have made and continue to make.

Yeah, yeah...we know.

You might be thinking,

"Wait a second! I thought this was a self-help book! I thought this was supposed to make me feel good about myself so that I can get more things done, manage my time better, and stop wasting money!"

And it is - but the first step to changing and getting help is admitting that you have a problem.

So if you're still wearing your Busy Badge, say this to yourself out loud:

"My busyness is a choice."

If you didn't say it out loud or if you heard that little voice in your head say, *"That's stupid, I don't need to say this out loud..."* that's an even bigger reason to say it out loud.

Once you understand that your busyness is a choice, you are empowered to make positive changes to take control of your life and stop being so busy, unproductive and unfulfilled.

So if you didn't say it out loud, let's try this again:

"My busyness is a CHOICE."

There.

Doesn't that feel better?

Even a little bit?

Take a deep breath and pat yourself on the back.

You're on the road to recovery.

CHAPTER 2: Dreams, Visions and Goals, Oh My!

"Crystallize your goals. Make a plan for achieving them and set yourself a deadline. Then, with supreme confidence, determination and disregard for obstacles and other people's criticisms, carry out your plan."

— Paul J. Meyer

As we talk with people about time management, efficiency and planning, we find that many are missing a very significant piece to cracking the puzzle of realizing their dreams.

What is that missing piece?

Actually choosing a goal!

It sounds so simple, but very few people actually do this!

Where do you want to go?

What does your big picture look like?

What are your dreams?

What are your goals?

Do you know the difference between the two?

And lastly, how do you plan all of this out and take action that will lead to the realization of those dreams and goals?

We are going to help you find your path, set your direction and design the life that you want to live.

The process is not hard, but it takes some soul searching on your part.

As we stated in chapter one, you have found yourself at this moment in time with the circumstances that you are in based on choices that you have made thus far.

You are now at a crossroads...and it's time to get to work!

At this time, please complete worksheet 2A

Please take some time to think about and fill out the first worksheet - it's a great starting point for the rest of the book.

The key here is to isolate the answer to what it is that you want to change as well as what it is that you really love to do.

Once you've done that, the hard part is figuring out how to do what you love and work towards the change you are seeking.

If you are feeling fulfilled doing what you love, making life changes that you desire are much more simple.

Here are some other questions to consider after filling the worksheet out:

Does your life and the decisions you make on a regular basis leave you feeling fulfilled or fear-filled?

If you do desire to change where you currently are, what is it that you are seeking or missing?

Do you even know yet?

Are you passionate about the current job, project or business that you are working on?

Does your current job, project or business have you constantly exhausted or constantly engaged and excited?

Now take a few minutes (or more than a few minutes) thinking about what makes you feel alive - what leaves you feeling fulfilled?

Please complete worksheet 2B

Now that you've filled these forms out, you've got a guidepost for achieving your goals in a way that will leave you feeling fulfilled instead of burnt out!

By figuring out what it is that keeps you going throughout the day, you've got a huge clue to the types of things you should strongly consider going after more intentionally.

Those things that you wake up excited about? These things are the things that we would recommend pursuing no matter how hard it can get sometimes.

You now have the choice of whether or not you are going to pursue those things that will make you feel engaged, alive, and hopeful about your future.

We understand that you may not be able to just up and leave your job today and that you can't always just turn on a dime to make certain changes.

That is not what this is about. This is about getting ready to lay down some goals and establishing a plan to achieve those goals.

Understand that some things that you think are dreams are actually goals and vice versa.

Let's lay some quick groundwork here to help you understand the differences.

A dream is wanting to own a home free and clear.

A goal is wanting to own a 4 bedroom home in Salem, Oregon with a white picket fence, an in-ground pool, paying $100,000 or less *in full* with no need for a mortgage - all within the next five years.

A dream is wanting to be able to not have a full time job working for someone else - but instead working for yourself and building your own business.

A goal is wanting to work for yourself as an architect that designs commercial real estate buildings and earning six figures or more per year - by January of 2019.

Another dream is to be able to pay for your children's education.

But a goal? That would be having $80,000+ in savings by December of 2020 so that your child can attend the liberal arts school that she wants to without needing to go into debt.

Maybe you'd like to take your spouse on that Caribbean cruise that you have always talked about.

The goal would be establishing the specifics of that dream - setting aside $5,000 by the end of the year so you can purchase the tickets from some specific travel agent to go on some specific cruise.

Do you see the difference?

Dreams are oftentimes somewhat general - while goals need to be specific, measurable, and usually have numbers and dates attached to them.

No matter how big or how small, dreams are really the stuff that goals are made of. Goals are the specifics of those dreams.

So many of us have become so absorbed with our day to day lives that we have forgotten what it was like to dream.

If no one else has, allow us to give you permission to DREAM again!

Have you had trouble jump-starting your dream engine?

One way to get out of a funk like that is to try "vision casting".

What is vision casting?

Vision casting is seeing yourself at a moment in time in the future and imagining what your life will be like in that moment.

This is where you take your vision casting worksheets (marked 2C in your workbook) and some time to put your imagination and your dreams to work.

With the sheets next to you, use the next few paragraphs as a guide to get started.

This is where you'll need to allow yourself to dream again. Think about what you will have accomplished between now and then - and what you really want to see yourself doing.

This can take 5 minutes or 5 days to figure out. The first time Lany did a vision casting session it took her three days of thinking, dreaming and sleeping on it to really be able to see the dream and the vision in her head.

Please don't rush through this section of the book or skip over it just because you want to keep reading.

If you feel the temptation to do so, ask yourself simply, *"Why am I reading this in the first place?"*

We structured this very specifically so that you could get the maximum amount of *awesome* injected into your life...and a huge part of that is being able to crush through those mental barriers that prevent people from painting a picture of the life of their dreams in their mind first.

Remember to take your time, there is no rush. There is also is no right or wrong answer here.

When you think about your vision, try to keep these 6 different aspects in mind: Spiritual, Family, Business, Health, Philanthropy and Finances.

Consider writing headers for each aspect in order of importance; this will help you focus and be very specific as you dream.

You don't have to write this out exactly as we have suggested, but we have found it to be a great place to start. You may have other aspects that you'd like to focus on instead, for example.

Below is a *short* example of a vision casting session from Ryan:

"It is the end of the first day of January in 2019, and wow what a year it has been!

I spent the last six months around the mountains of Tibet and connecting with some of the most interesting and humble people that I have ever met. They have shown me things about what it means to enjoy the little things in life that I never could have learned anywhere else.

Before that, my wife and I had the privilege of spending a month with close family members in Europe backpacking through areas that I had only previously seen on postcards and in the movies.

If it hadn't been for making the decision to work for ourselves, we never would have had this kind of financial and geographic freedom. Our business has never been doing better - we have clients all around the world and have been booked solid for over two years now.

We finally have the freedom to really choose what clients we want to work with because our services are in such high demand. Actually, ever since we published *Stop Wasting Time and Burning Money*, our lives took a massively positive upward turn.

We were able to spend as much time with our family as we wanted to because of the decisions we made to focus on building our own brands and businesses instead of working at a job we hated just so we could have some temporary "stability".

Our job security comes from knowing that we do excellent work with an amazing network of wonderful people who now surround and champion us everywhere that we go.

Since we were able to pay off all of our nagging debts from student loans and old business deals, we have had so much more peace of mind and the finances to fund the things we really want to do - like building schools and orphanages in countries less fortunate than our own.

Next month we'll be opening our fifteenth orphanage in Kenya. FIFTEENTH!

Those kids are why we do what we do - there is nothing in the world like their smiles and the hugs they give when we visit.

Knowing that we're now able to help give them the love and care that they need despite the tough lives they've had makes all the pain and struggle it took to get to this place all worth it.

It's hard to believe that just five years ago we were so convinced we'd never get out of the hole we were in - and now here we are feeling like we're on top of the world. Life is a funny thing sometimes.

We remind ourselves often how thankful we are and spend as much time as we can enjoying each other's company and having fun with our friends and family. It helps to remember where we've come from so that we know how to help others who have been where we were.

Time for bed now - we start production on our second feature film tomorrow!"

With that in mind, and with as much detail as you can muster, answer the following questions:

First, pick a date 5 years from now.

It can be your birthday, a holiday or any other date as long as it is 5 years from the year that you are in.

What do you want that day to look like from beginning to end?

No limits. No fear. No self-limiting bullshit.

Use your wildest imagination and let yourself dream again!

Write your response to the question on the vision casting worksheets. It's okay if you need more paper, just print out as many of the worksheets as you need.

Fill out the worksheets marked 2C: Vision Casting

Once you have your vision complete, read it back to yourself!

It feels good, doesn't it? To allow your imagination and your dreams to work together and paint a picture for you of what life could look like if you let out all the stops and went after what you're passionate about?

Even writing this section of the book was a massive exercise in vision-casting for us!

We would suggest that you keep those vision-casting sheets in a place where you will see them regularly and read them as often as you need to.

You will want to keep them in the forefront of your mind so you can stay focused on the path to making those dreams a reality.

The old adage, "Out of sight, out of mind" really can apply to just about anything, especially when it comes to the fulfillment of the life you want for yourself and your loved ones.

It is always a good idea to update, refresh, adjust or renew your vision each year whether it be on the anniversary date of the original writing or the first of the year.

Sometimes even the best planned plans just don't pan out...so it is a good idea to be flexible on some things, but if there is something that is really important to you, do whatever it takes to make that dream a reality!

Keep your dreams safe!

One of the hardest things about navigating the path to fulfilling your dreams is that there are inevitably a ton of naysayers who will try to distract and dissuade you from going after them.

We've all been there - you get a new idea or something that you want to do and the first thing you do is tell some friends of yours. For whatever reason, those friends aren't the most supportive and they end up telling you all the reasons that your idea is a bad idea.

Maybe they are projecting their own fears or insecurities onto you.

Maybe they are bored with their own lives and get frustrated when they see someone who is excited about the future.

Whatever it may be, you've got to keep your dreams safe from those 'dream killers'!

Think of your new vision casting sheets as a seed or a small child that you need to protect and nurture until it grows up and can stand on its own.

Make sure to share your dreams with those that are like-minded and who will support you on the journey that you are embarking upon. Find a group of people who will walk and even run that journey with you!

It makes it all that much more enjoyable.

Once you have kicked the naysayers out, given the boot to the dream killers and surrounded yourself with a protective layer of support, you can really start making your dreams a reality. This will take time, energy, and hard decisions to set healthy boundaries for yourself and your loved ones. Just know that from the start and you won't be surprised!

"A goal without a plan is just a wish." - Antoine de Saint-Exupéry

---

Please understand something...

If this were easy, everyone would be doing it.

Don't quit when it gets hard. It will. You can be sure of that. Always remember why you got started in the first place.

Your next step is to define how and when you want to achieve that dream. This is where goal setting comes into play.

Again, you will need to go to your worksheets for this.

Take a look at the vision casting worksheet that you completed.

Soon we will ask you to take some time to break down the individual dreams that are within worksheet 2C into actual goals on the "SMART" goals worksheet 2D.

If you need more space, feel free to print out extra copies of worksheet 2D.

No matter what your dream is, we suggest making sure that your goals fit into what is often called a "SMART" goal. If you haven't heard the term, here's quick refresher course:

SMART goals are Specific, Measurable, Attainable, Relevant, and Time-bound.

As you go through this worksheet, make sure to ask yourself if what you are writing down fits into the above five categories.

If your goal does not meet the criteria then we would advise adjusting it to make sure that it does.

For example, if your dream is to help your spouse retire early from their job then write down what it will take to do just that.

What steps do you need to make?

How many sales do you have to close?

How many new business partners do you need to bring into your business?

How many prospects do you need to talk to each day?

What do you need to be making and by what date in order to achieve that goal?

These are all the types of questions you should be asking yourself so that you can get really specific with your goal-setting.

If dreams are the skeleton, then goal-setting is the muscles that will help "flesh out" those dreams to becoming reality.

Taking the time to fill out your worksheets will help you immensely in turning arbitrary ideas and dreams into something concrete: a plan that you can follow until you arrive at the desired destination.

In the next chapter, we will help you through the implementation of the goals you have set.

Fill out worksheet 2D before moving on

CHAPTER 3: Working Your Plan

"If you fail to plan, you plan to fail."

— Benjamin Franklin

Take a moment and think about this quote from Ben Franklin.

Obviously, no one is planning to fail on purpose!

The issue is that many people simply neglect to set a plan in place that will help them achieve the goals they desire so deeply.

Now that you have your dreams written out along with the concrete 'SMART' goals, you're at the point where plugging these things into your daily life is the most important thing you can do.

This is where you'll build a plan and develop a strategy that works for you.

One of the hardest things for a lot of people is getting a handle on their time - despite the fact that we are all given the same amount of it in a day.

We include ourselves in this!

By scheduling the steps you need to accomplish your goals into an actual calendar (and obviously following through on those steps), you will see your goals realized much faster.

This really isn't rocket science!

Have you ever wondered why certain people seem to be able to get so many things done while others just seem to be floating through their day?

Of all of the high-performing leaders we have worked with and studied, we have found that one of the main things they have in common is this: *they plan their work schedule instead of letting their work load dictate their day.*

This is not easy - but once you get in the habit of deciding your schedule, you will amaze yourself at how much you can accomplish.

Everyone will have a different system - the key here is to just start figuring out the kind of calendar system that works for you.

If you don't have some kind of calendar system for yourself, accomplishing the things you want to accomplish will become much more difficult.

We believe that success comes from doing the really important things that are critical to obtaining the results you desire.

This is an issue of deciding what your priorities are and making the (sometimes difficult) decision of sticking to them when you've got a thousand other things clamoring for your attention.

All the goals and dreams that you write down will amount to little if you don't figure out a way to actually implement the action-steps needed to accomplish them...and setting a schedule for yourself is one of the most efficient ways we have found to do so.

So...pull out your calendar!

It can be on your computer, your second screen or an actual physical paper calendar. We use all of the above for different reasons.

Are you not used to using a calendar or don't have one that you like?

There's no time like the present to learn, adjust, and grow!

The DayPlanner company makes great calendars for people in all walks of life and business.

You can pick up a planner or a calendar from just about any retail store these days.

This is an exercise in prioritizing what is important to you.

We want to help you get your priorities straight.

You will never hear someone on their death bed saying that they regretted not working more or spending less time with their families and friends.

With how busy all of us can get, it can be easy to forget the reasons we started this journey in the first place - which is usually because we want a better life for us and our loved ones to share together.

So let's take a look at the month that you are in right now.

We can't recommend highly enough that you make it a point to block out all of your family and personal time on the calendar.

Yes, this means family dinners, church functions, birthday parties, vacations, movie nights, kids events, sports, etc.

Consider color coding your calendars, whether it is digital or physical. These blocked out family times should be viewed as **not negotiable** from now on, barring a robot or zombie apocalypse.

Even if the world is falling apart around you, do your best to make it a point to stick to hanging out with your loved ones as much as possible.

You won't regret it!

When you are booking your business or other life events in your calendar, they should be scheduled **around** your life, not the other way around.

We work to live, we don't live to work!

Even if you're not sure what all those family/friend events are right now (no one ever is), it's a good habit to just start blocking certain times out of your day that are specifically marked as "FAMILY TIME".

Once you've done that, even if it is just for the next week, sit back for a moment and think about how this makes you feel!

You just made a choice to put your family and personal life first.

Your loved ones will LOVE this and the quality of your life is certain to improve.

Don't let any feelings of guilt try to sneak in here. Family should always come first. **Always**.

The more you are willing to work through this process and the more often you do so, the easier it becomes.

Print out a few copies of worksheet 3A

This sheet will help you break down the actionable steps you need to take in order to realize a specific goal.

Feel free to print out as many copies of this worksheet as you need.

Keep in mind that this list should not have a bunch of things on it that don't somehow line up with the goals and dreams that you've already established.

This is just an exercise to help break down achieving your goals into actionable tasks.

Once you've got those actionable tasks broken down for each goal, then you'll want to put those things into your calendar so you can make sure you actually get them done!

One way that we manage our schedule is creating blocks of time on certain days for certain things.

For example, every Wednesday, Lany has an event that she has to participate in. This event runs from 9 AM until almost noon, so she blocks out her morning until noon and eliminates all distractions from this part of her schedule.

There is no negotiating on this block of time - and making that kind of powerful decision will have a profound effect on your productivity.

If you are working a regular job and you had someone ask you to go to the movies between the hours of 9:00 AM and 5:00 PM, would it even be a possibility?

Probably not, unless you have the coolest boss in the world!

Try to think of the events you're scheduling in your calendar like that - because this stuff does take work, after all!

Being able to schedule certain events several weeks in advance does help make the transition into a more disciplined lifestyle easier.

If you look at our calendars, they look like coloring books. All of the different tasks on our calendars are highlighted in different colors for different topics and goals.

We do our best to break down each block of time to the specific tasks that will help us accomplish our goals.

Lany even schedules sleep, workouts, devotional time and meals.

Everything!

It may seem ridiculous or even excessive, but it really does work especially when you are just starting out or making some dramatic adjustments to your lifestyle.

Make an effort to do this regularly in order to keep your time in check.

Here's the bizarre thing about all of this:

Once you are used to living on a schedule that *you* decide, it becomes easy. Life becomes more manageable because you're doing the managing instead of life managing you.

You will find that you have more time to get things done.

Your stress level will decrease and you can start to enjoy your life even more.

The hardest part of all of this is figuring out a system that works for you and your personality style.

Obviously you don't need to take everything we say here as "the way it is", because everyone is different. We are just sharing things that we know to work personally because it is how we conduct our daily lives.

You may find you like using a physical calendar much more than a digital one.

We like the digital ones because it is much easier to set reminders to keep us on track.

You may find that you don't like scheduling meal times and prefer to leave large blocks of "free space" in your calendar.

It's really all up to you. This book is not a magic wand that is going to fix all of your problems - we just wanted to share with the world the methods we have found helpful.

These kind of extreme changes are not going to happen overnight - and the sooner you recognize that, the easier it will be to be patient with yourself.

As we mentioned in chapter 1, you have to first recognize that your current behavior and the choices you make play a major part in why things aren't the way you want them to be right now.

Admitting that is not easy for a lot of people.

We have done our best to provide the worksheets with this book that will help shine some light on what's actually going on and how you're currently operating.

If you really want things to change, you've got to address the behavior, the mindsets, and the choices that are leading to your current results.

If you don't like the results you're getting, make a commitment to change the behavior that brings those negative results.

Being open to new processes and ways of doing things will help you immensely.

Implement those new processes and see what works for you. Trying to do all of it at once will most likely overwhelm you - so give yourself grace to ease into things.

Follow through and know that if you really want something to become a habit, it will take about a month of regular practice. Studies show that you really begin to form new habits after 30 days of regular practice (or 40 minutes per day).

(If you'd like more information about ways to learn faster, check out this video on the Reformation Designs YouTube channel[1].)

Don't give up even when you make a mistake or forget to schedule something.

For example, eventually you won't need to schedule your sleep and your meals, as you will learn to leave space in your calendar for those things.

Until then, we recommend that you schedule out every hour of your day so you can see where your time is spent.

It is a very educational and eye-opening process.

You will really figure out where you spend your time, how you operate your business and what you are doing with your life.

Some people function very well with daily to-do lists.

On the flip side and as an example of something different, blogger Pat Flynn of SmartPassiveIncome.com[2] has an alternative system instead of a daily to-do list.

---

[1]https://www.youtube.com/watch?v=tqoiFWThugU

[2]http://www.smartpassiveincome.com

He recommends coming up with to-do lists for each *project* that you're working on and dedicating a specific amount of time each day to focusing on individual projects.

Whatever it is that you end up doing, you will figure out a system that works for you as you go along.

As we have said, the suggestions in this book are simply that - suggestions.

Can you stick with your productivity plan for at least 1 month? We would love to hear from you!

Make sure to contact one of us and let us know about your struggles, your successes, and anything you learned along the way.

Also, if you'd like a much more detailed example of how to schedule your day, check out the book "Brainshare" by Joe Siecinski[3].

In the next chapter, we're going to talk about how to nail down those distractions and focus on the things that will actually make you money!

---

[3] http://goo.gl/6HTa9V

CHAPTER 4: Time Management, Distractions, & IPAs

"He who every morning plans the transactions of that day and follows that plan carries a thread that will guide him through the labyrinth of the most busy life."

— Victor Hugo

If you're still on board, good!

In this chapter, we're going to talk about time management, dealing with distractions, and IPAs.

And no, we don't mean the beer! IPA is short for "Income Producing Activities."

Keep in mind as you read this chapter that we suggest you dedicate at least an hour for what you're about to read and do.

This is another one of the more interactive chapters in the book and we have included some more worksheets to help you out.

As with the other worksheets, understand that they will involve some time and reflection on your part to really achieve optimal results.

Time Management

We have already established that time management is all about choices...and that those choices are made by you, whether subconsciously or not.

A lot of people mistakenly will assume that the reason that they have such a hard time staying productive is because of a lack of proper resources or tools - and while that may be a small factor, the core issue is understanding how to break through mental barriers and make healthier choices.

Are there amazing tools that will make your life and business run more efficiently?

Absolutely. And we will share a lot of those with you later on - but the hard work here starts with laying a strong foundation. How do you do that?

By recognizing that YOU ultimately choose where and how you spend your time and putting the work in that's involved with figuring out how to make better decisions.

It's time to talk about your to-do list - the things that you need to do, the things you want to do, and everything in between that you probably write down somewhere.

The next worksheet is where you'll make a prioritized list of the top ten most important things that you've got to get done right now.

Feel free to include everyday items like picking up the kids from school, etc...but also keep in mind that your goals won't accomplish themselves!

Make sure to add some of those action steps to your list!

Please fill out worksheet 4A

Great job! Next we are going to look at your *distractions.*

This is going to be an accountability session with yourself.

Here is where you'll make a list of your distractions. Make this as FULL a list as possible.

Do not leave anything out - as this is predominantly an exercise in being real with yourself about the things that you do to avoid the stuff you want to get done.

Here are a few examples:

Endlessly browsing social media, video games, television, doing laundry, dishes, family drama, auto repairs, radio, internet, excessive drinking, organizing paperwork, cleaning, etc.

Keep in mind - there is nothing inherently wrong with any of these things or doing them as long as they're done in moderation.

By moderation, we mean that you're not using them as an escape hatch to avoid the work involved in accomplishing your goals!

Everyone has stuff to deal with sometimes and important tasks come up that need to be taken care of.

And of course, you've got to get the laundry done ESPE-CIALLY if you want to have clean underwear.

The point of this exercise is to start looking at what YOU get distracted by.

This is about asking yourself:

What am I CHOOSING to do instead of what actually needs to be done?

There are some things on all of our to do lists that we will do ANYTHING to keep from doing.

And we do mean anything, right down to organizing paperwork or reading all the bad news in the popular media... and man, do we HATE paperwork and fear-mongering news media with a passion!

What is it that makes us choose to do something else over what needs to be done?

Sometimes it is fear of the item on the to do list.

Yes, just like you, we are sometimes (*read: most times*) afraid or unsure of the projects that we are working on, so we find ways to work around it - WAY around it!

This does none of us any good at all, obviously.

It only hurts us and feeds our own fear or insecurity.

Would you like a simple way to re-frame your thinking when you are dealing with distractions and avoiding things that you may be putting off intentionally?

Think about how good you end up feeling after you finally get done procrastinating and conquer that thing that's been nagging you.

When you catch yourself procrastinating and doing menial tasks or distracting things instead of the stuff you know you need and want to get done, remember that feeling of accomplishment and it makes it much easier to push through.

Also, if there are certain things that you absolutely must get accomplished in a day that won't really take you much time to do, try doing those first to get some momentum going.

We all know what it is like when you hit that magic place that people call "the zone". Steven Kotler calls it "flow". Whatever you call it, it is in those moments that you do your best work.

Sometimes the easiest way to get in the zone is to use those small tasks that take up brain space as leverage to springboard yourself into doing the things you really want to be doing.

This technique should help you overcome some of those distractions you are about to write down.

We would suggest keeping this list in a prominent place where you often try to get your work done - perhaps in your office, next to your computer, in your study, etc.

When you feel that familiar procrastination monster breathing down your neck, take a look at the list and figure out what it is that you're doing and why.

Sometimes all it takes is seeing "mindlessly scrolling on social media" on that distraction worksheet to snap Ryan out of it!

Goodbye endless Facebook noise and drama; hello productivity and clear-mindedness!

What do you do on your distraction list that is taking you away from your actual to do list?

Why are you choosing the distraction over the important item?

Is the distraction hurting or helping you?

What is the core issue behind why you default to doing the things that distract you?

These are just some questions that can help snap you out of that zone.

With that said...

Please fill out worksheet 4B

Now that you have made your priorities list and been honest with yourself about the things that distract you, take a few minutes and put the book down...but bring the list of 'important things' with you.

Leave your distractions list somewhere else as a symbolic gesture of you pursuing the things that matter most to you and walking away from what's not really important.

Maybe go outside or go to a different room in your house - just change the scenery and get a glass of water or something.

When you're looking at your list, ask yourself these questions:

How important are the things on this list, and are they really prioritized properly?

Am I making sure to include at least one actionable task towards my goals in this to-do list?

Go ahead - take your list and reflect for a few minutes.

Now that you've taken some time to really make sure that the items on your list are the important ones, you may want to organize your thoughts a bit more.

We have provided several different types of worksheets to help you out here.

You may want to make a variety of different to-do lists and organize them by when you want to get them done.

Some ideas to think about would be a list of things you need to do, things you want to do, and maybe even a list of things you'd like to do but know they need to be back burner items.

Fill out worksheets 4C - 4G as you see fit

These worksheets are broken down by things you need to get done today, this week, this month, and this year. We also included a list for you to write down things that you want to do but might need to postpone until a later time.

These are for you to use as often as you would like for whatever projects you choose.

The most important thing that we suggest focusing on is *breaking your lists down to the few items that you have to get done now* and to not overwhelm yourself trying to accomplish everything at once.

Pick a specific goal and work on it until it's finished. As simple as this sounds, ask yourself honestly:

"Do I do this?"

Everyone struggles with this issue, so don't beat yourself up about it if you don't. But being aware of the need to break things down to smaller steps is incredibly important and is most of the battle.

As corny as it might sound, every journey does truly begin with the first step. How much time and energy do we spend thinking *about* doing something instead of actually just sitting down and doing it?

Setting a goal of "being good at playing the piano" is really vague and can feel overwhelming. But committing to just 20 minutes a day when you first wake up to start learning to play piano? Over time, that will lead to massive progress.

Telling yourself that you'll spend a short amount of time per day working on that goal of yours is the easiest way to overcome the feeling of utter hopelessness that can come swooping in. You know which one we mean right? The one that shows up the moment you realize that you don't know how to do what it is that you're setting out to do?

Try to imagine yourself in the role of a dragon-slayer - and that goal is your dragon. It never attacks you, but it is loud and taunts you often - telling you that you'll never be able to defeat it.

Then imagine that every time you work on achieving that goal that you're wearing down the creature's defenses until eventually you master it.

If that kind of imagination helps you achieve your real life goals, why not have fun with it?

(If the idea of that sounds even remotely interesting to you, check out habitica.com - it is a great application that makes productivity into a game.)

This will take time. It will take patience. It will take discipline...but the reward is worth the work required to obtain it.

Sometimes it really is as simple as just choosing to get started.

It becomes much more simple to do the other things on your to-do lists once you've got a bit of momentum going - and especially once you get the satisfaction of knowing you've accomplished some things that are really important to you.

...but now here is the really hard question. And we ask it regardless of whether or not you would consider yourself an entrepreneur - because we feel it is important enough to ask hard questions that encourage critical thinking.

Do the items on your to do list(s) make you money?

Are they what some folks like to call income producing activities (IPA's)?

...or are they just time vacuums - producing no lasting valuable good in your life but taking energy away from you, your loved ones and the dreams you're building together?

This is a question that you've got to seriously ask yourself if you want to get to a point where you really "stop wasting time and burning money", as it were.

We are not saying that money is the most important thing in the world. What we are saying is that once you start thinking seriously about the things you spend your time doing, you'll find that a lot of that time is spent doing frivolous things that don't help move you forward towards the goals that you have set for yourself.

Your lists will be helpful to figure out exactly the kinds of things that you are doing that take up your time, but asking the above question about the items on your list will really be the great equalizer.

Here are some other hard-hitting questions to get you thinking:

- *"Is spending all this time on social media going to make me money in the long run?"*
- *"Are those countless hours of watching TV/YouTube/Netflix or binging on Game of Thrones really adding anything positive to my life that will help me construct the life that I dream of...or is it just COSTING me money at the end of the day because of all the time I'm wasting?"*
- *"Is checking my e-mail a dozen times in a day helping me accomplish what I want to do, or helping to accomplish someone else's agenda instead?"*

If what you're doing is not an income producing activity and it is still a "must do" on your to do list, then you may want to have a conversation with yourself and find out if it must stay and why.

We're not talking about everyday things like making sure that your family is well-fed or your children are picked up from school.

We mean the types of things that you find yourself doing every day that are mostly just distractions from you realizing your goals.

Again, you are the powerful one here. You get to choose where each task falls. Your choices have brought you to this current moment.

Ask yourself, *"is doing this going to help me create the wealth and income that I need to live the kind of life that I want?"*

Asking that is a good way to get your brain back on track when you're dealing with any number of incessant distractions.

This is an exercise that you may want to run through quite often.

If you do it enough, it will eventually become like second nature and you will find yourself marveling at how you ever functioned differently.

You'll also find yourself wondering how other people function in any way OTHER than the way you're living!

Like we've said elsewhere and will continue to say, however - make sure to give yourself grace on all of this stuff.

You are human, after all - so learning to be patient and loving towards yourself even when you're not "getting everything done" is all part of the process.

You will still get distracted and you will still procrastinate, just like everyone else.

It's just the way it is.

Our goal is just to equip you with tools, perspective, and ideas that will help you accomplish what you set your mind to.

Both of us have projects that we've yet to start because mentally, we're just not prepared to pursue them.

That will happen at times, and that's okay.

Sometimes you will have grandiose plans and ideas and think that you must push forward but the timing seems off.

That is not a distraction or procrastination.

That is wisdom. Tune in to it!

...but what about relaxing?

We're glad you asked!

Sometimes the healthiest thing you can do to give yourself a break from working and just go have fun! Many of us in our culture struggle with feeling guilty for not getting enough done because of the way our workforce is structured.

People are used to being punished for not producing enough. Sometimes they can feel like if they stop to take the time to rest and relax that they might be seen as lazy or not good enough.

That is nonsense.

We work to live, we don't live to work!

(More on this in Charlie Hoehn's amazing book, Play It Away[4] *for those of you who are burnt out from working too darn hard!)*

The point of this book is *not* to create more workaholics that never have time for anything enjoyable or fun - it is to help you get better at achieving what is really important in your life!

That is, to help you harness your abilities to do what you WANT to do and simultaneously become more efficient doing the things you NEED to do.

As long as you understand that this process will take *time* and *energy* and *work*, it will be easier for you to navigate through the inevitable obstacles that will arise.

You will find what works for you and what doesn't.

It will just require practice, application and patience.

And practice.

And more practice.

---

[4]http://goo.gl/0GTd0W

CHAPTER 5: Instant Overnight Success

"Timing, perseverance, and ten years of trying will eventually make you look like an overnight success."

— Biz Stone, co-founder of Twitter

Regardless of how many "overnight successes" you see on YouTube or in the media, there's one thing you've got to comprehend if you're going to stick out this productivity/entrepreneur thing for the long haul.

...and that is realizing that "overnight success" is a **LIE**.

Many people treat their success like they are playing the lottery...hoping that one day, eventually they'll just make it big.

Have you ever checked out the likelihood that you'll win the lottery?

On the flip side, if you spend any amount of time studying the lives and journeys of people throughout history who have had any measure of financial or entrepreneurial success, almost every single one of them will tell you the same thing.

Wrap your head around this one....

'SUCCESS' IS A PROCESS.

Step back, slow down and let's do a reality check!

The creative process for anyone is something that takes time, patience, and a ton of practice to master. The people who make it look easy are the same people who can tell you how many years of hard work, blood, sweat and tears they put into their craft.

It has been said of world-renown painter and sculptor Pablo Picasso that he was once approached by a woman in the marketplace.

"Mr Picasso," she said as she handed him a piece of paper. "I'm a big fan. Please, could you do a little drawing for me?"

Picasso smiled and created a piece of art for her on the paper provided.

Handing it back to her, he said, "That will be a million dollars."

"But Mr Picasso," she replied, "it took you only 30 seconds to do this little masterpiece."

"My good woman," Picasso laughed, *"it took me 30 years to do that masterpiece in 30 seconds."*

Let's be real here.

There's a good chance that only about 20% of you who read this will actually do something with the information and change your lives and habits for the better.

So, will you be one of the 20% who goes on to pursue the dreams and goals that are burning within you, or one of the 80% majority who do nothing?

Are you going to quit? Are you going to give up when things get hard?

Or are you going to, as Lany says, *"put on your big girl panties and get on with it"*?

You have to work for what you want. No one else is going to force you to manage your time better.

Just like us, you have to find what works for you. You have to develop your own systems and strategies and then learn how to tweak them as you go.

What works for Lany does not necessarily always work for Ryan and vice versa. It's okay that you have a different method and process.

Make your process work for you. Give yourself grace in knowing that *it is...a...process.*

If you're not sure where to start, try implementing the suggestions that we talked about in this book and follow through for the next 30 days.

If you can make the commitment to yourself to do this, you will see what works and what does not work. At the end of your 30 days you can make adjustments and fine tune your process for the next month. Of course, don't feel bad if you find that something simply doesn't work for you or your style.

Make sure to at least give a lot of the tools and systems a try for awhile before deciding it doesn't work for you.

Throughout this book we have given you the tools to build a solid foundation for a more productive life. This is about the big picture.

Time mastery does not just encompass filling up a calendar and lists of tasks.

There is a bigger picture to paint here - and it's called your future!

If you've had a difficult time moving forward, please understand that the chances are you will continue to run things into the ground until you figure out that *you're the powerful one that is in charge of the decisions you're making.*

You will have to wash, rinse, repeat until you nail down the process that works the best for you.

As you go through your week, evaluate what is working and what is not working.

We'd suggest getting a journal to keep track of how you you are doing. For example, at the end of each week, try grading yourself on a scale from 1-10 on how efficient you feel you were.

Take note of the days that you accomplished the things you really wanted to and do your best to figure out what you did differently on those days versus the days that you struggled.

Check your time spent on distractions vs. IPA's. Where are you spending most of your time?

Are you still spending too much time on your favorite distraction because you are avoiding working on that IPA that you are subconsciously afraid of?

Maybe consider putting aside that particular IPA for a later date and pick something else.

It may not be time to work on it, as we said earlier. This will also help you eliminate that distraction.

How did your time management line up with your goals for the week? Did you do everything you wanted to get done?

If not, understand that it is perfectly normal.

Change is not easy for anyone, and we wanted this book to be a manual to help ease you through the process and give you the encouragement that it's perfectly okay to make mistakes along the way.

You're the one who needs to learn how to manage your own expectations. Perhaps you set too lofty of a goal when you were just getting started - or maybe your goal wasn't challenging enough.

Your process should grow and evolve with you. What worked 15 years ago probably does not work today.

What worked one year ago may or may not work today.

It's okay to change. If you can accept that change is inevitable, then it will make this process that you go through much smoother.

We believe in you! We know that you can go through this process. Now, you need to have faith in yourself.

Stick to your plan and get out of your own way!

We can be our own biggest roadblocks sometimes. If you drift into self-sabotaging, ask yourself why?

Consider pulling out the worksheets again and going over *why* you got started in the first place.

"Most importantly, always remember your values. Remember the WHY...the reason why you got into it in the first place. Because it's inevitable, just like in life, entrepreneurs especially will go [through] ups and downs day and night. And in those down moments, if you don't think of the WHY, if you don't remember that, you'll stay down and never come back up again."

— Jenn Lim, CEO of Delivering Happiness in a June 3, 2013 interview[5]

You can do this!

Now that we're on the same page about the creative process, the next step is to learn about some of the countless tools that are available to help you along the way.

Of all of the books we have read and the business conferences we've attended, we have found it to be incredibly rare for many entrepreneurs to reveal the inner workings of their infrastructure...their "HOW" if you will.

We believe that everyone wins when people share how they achieved their goals.

---

[5]https://www.youtube.com/watch?v=un8fviaXSY0

We have done our best to include as many of the different tools and resources that we've come across that have helped us at one point or another.

Now dear reader, keep in mind that this is where this stuff can really start to be overwhelming. Especially if you wouldn't consider yourself even remotely tech-savvy.

There are so many apps, websites, and other resources out there that can help you with this or that.

How do you figure out what works best for you?

Testing, testing, and testing again!

Yes, you have to test it all. We have tried different tools for different aspects of our business and personal lives and we are constantly looking to improve.

The next chapter is chock-full of a whole bunch of them and is no means exhaustive.

You know best how you think, operate and function. We may think that a particular tool is amazing, but it doesn't matter until you put that tool to the test for you.

One of the best tricks we have implemented is to try out a tool for at least two weeks to find out if it will fit into your workflow.

You will know pretty quickly with some tools that they will not work at all for you and your endeavors.

Others need some time to develop the skills necessary to use them efficiently.

Some of the resources we provide are paid services, but most of them also have free trials available. Check them out (and actually use the trials) to see if they work for you.

Don't get stuck on your favorite tools.

Be open minded when other people make new recommendations.

Companies are constantly developing new apps and programs to make our lives easier. There is always a chance that there is a new program that will be better than one you are currently using.

And yes, this is a lot of work.

We never said this would be easy, but it is worth it in the long run!

CHAPTER 6 -
Infrastructure & Resources

"Do not wait; the time will never be 'just right.' Start where you stand, and work with whatever tools you may have at your command, and better tools will be found as you go along."

— George Herbert

We have mentioned a few times throughout this book that as entrepreneurs, we have been frustrated by the glaring lack of others who have come before us that have actually shared their infrastructure.

What do we mean by infrastructure?

We're talking about their "how to" - the way they have set up their businesses on a practical level - not just a theoretical one full of hype and big promises that you'll be successful if you buy their programs and books.

There are certainly exceptions to this in the "self-help" world, but at least at the time of this writing, we do not feel it is the norm.

We are not afraid of our readers taking the information we share and using it to help them move forward in their lives or businesses - nor are we intimidated by the thought that yes, *even you may do something bigger and better than us!*

In fact, we **hope** that you take this information and use it to the best of your ability!

We hope that you end up becoming best-selling authors, speakers, coaches, and any number of other things.

We dare you - just give it a go and see what happens when you go after your dreams!

That being said, this chapter is all about the tools, resources, and techniques that you can use to structure your life and business endeavors.

It is by no means an exhaustive list - but we have done our best to compile enough to get you started (and in some cases, you'll probably feel overwhelmed by the sheer volume of them).

Also keep in mind that depending on when you are reading this, some of the tools may have changed, evolved, or been purchased by larger companies acquisitions teams.

The fact is that there are so many efficiency tools and re-sources on the market today - far more than ever before.

They are ever changing and ever improving because many of them have become sizable companies with incredibly intelligent engineers and employees bringing their best to the table every day.

This is a blessing and a curse. What may be here today may not be tomorrow, but on the flip side; what is here today may be very improved upon tomorrow.

You will have to do your own research for the tools that will best fit the needs of your business and your life.

The tools listed here are either tools that we use on a regular basis or we know that there are others who have become much more efficient by using them.

We have provided some links to third party reviews of some of these tools as well, so you can experience a few different perspectives. Ultimately, our biggest suggestion is to do your own research and look into the tools for yourself in order to see what will work best for you and your needs.

General "Must Have" Tools

EVERNOTE

Let's start with Evernote.

To put it simply, Evernote helps you keep track of all your notes.

Simple and straight forward, right? Well, yes and no.

You can use Evernote to save anything that you can imagine.

You can even use it as a CRM tool (customer relationship management).

You can organize all of it by notebooks and tags to help you sort anything you need to.

Evernote is also a great place to put all the websites, links, recipes, photos, articles and spreadsheets that you haven't known what to do with.

We cannot recommend highly enough if you pick up Evernote to also get their "Web Clipper" extension here[6].

It works directly within your browser window so that you can save entire web pages in one or two clicks to your Evernote account.

There is no way to elaborate on everything about Evernote here - but our friend Jason Frasca has written a great book that goes into a lot more detail!

---

[6]http://evernote.com/webclipper/

You can pick up Jason's book *Evernote Success* here[7].

There is a free version of Evernote as well as a premium version that gives you access to more features.

You can try Evernote by visiting their website at Evernote.com.

- Evernote has desktop and mobile compatibility.

- Chrome Extension available

---

[7]http://jmf.im/evernotesuccess

GOOGLE DRIVE

Google Drive is essentially a cloud version of Microsoft Office without the high cost, and is based entirely in your web browser or on various mobile applications.

Not only can you share it with other people on your team or in your family, but you can also choose the level of access that each person has.

For example, if you want someone to be able to view a document you're working on and leave feedback, but not be able to edit the original document, you can restrict access to only allow comments.

Access to any one document does not mean you give someone access to all of your files.

Just make sure to pay close attention to what you're sharing and who you're sharing it with!

One of our favorite features of Google Drive is the ability to collaborate with others in real time!

This is particularly awesome because, for example, you can write an entire book with your co-author who lives in another state at the exact same time!

When we compiled the majority of this book, Lany would write out her thoughts in one chapter while Ryan was working on formatting and adding his thoughts in other chapters.

The collaboration that can take place with Google Drive is unlike anything we've seen - because for the most part, it's all free, fast and reliable!

You can create spreadsheets, documents, forms, presentations, surveys, and various other things.

The best part is that all of it can be accessed anywhere that you have an internet connection and you can work with your team all over the world in real time on the same documents.

We have thousands of documents and pictures on Google Drive.

Despite how amazing all of our technology is these days, sometimes things do happen and servers go down, data is corrupted, things get hacked, etc.

That said, you also want to make sure that you regularly back up your data in more places than just on Google Drive and that you use strong passwords.

Passwords like "password123!" don't cut it anymore. Passwords should look more like this: "Dk@11Ac*!loPzSid$"

Good old fashioned little black books work great for keeping track of all the passwords.

So definitely make it a point to save your important data in more places than one!

We wrote the majority of this book together in Google Drive before we began finalizing it for print and E-Book distribution.

What you're reading right now would not be possible without Google Drive - so definitely check it out and see what you can do!

Try Google Drive here[8].

- Google Drive has desktop and mobile compatibility.

- Chrome Extension available

---

[8]http://drive.google.com

INSTAPAPER

Let's change gears a bit here and talk about all this content that you run across daily that you don't have time to read and all these websites that you have bookmarked.

We find ourselves bookmarking websites and links that we wanted to go back and look at or share from, but always lose the links in a massively overgrown list of bookmarks.

We're pretty sure that if you're reading this book that you can relate!

Here comes Instapaper to save the day! Lany thinks we need to give Instapaper it's own super-hero costume!

Instapaper is a "read later" app that allows to you to send your articles to your Kindle Device, save to your desktop app, read on your mobile app and also share with your social media platforms.

Here are a few articles from Lifehacker about Instapaper.[9]

Lany uses Instapaper every day and then once a week or so she will go through and read any articles that she has saved.

She can then decide to save them in designated folders for future use or delete them and move on.

There are many other "read later" apps that you can look into, but InstaPaper is one of the best in our opinion.

Try InstaPaper here.[10]

- InstaPaper has desktop, mobile & Kindle compatibility.

- Chrome Extension available

---

[9]http://bit.ly/1lvPBnf

[10]http://www.instapaper.com

Project Management

TRELLO

Evernote and Google Drive are great tools for saving and creating content.

The issue that both of us had was finding a good "Project Management" tool.

There are some really good ones out there, but none quite like Trello.

Think of Trello as a software that lets you create really organized sticky notes that you can drag and drop anywhere you'd like.

Trello gives you the ability to see a whole project from start to finish in one glance.

You have the option to create and manage several projects or boards at once and can collaborate with other people on your team as well.

The Lifehacker blog had some great reviews of Trello that you can find here with an excerpt below.[11]

> "Essentially, you set up the lists shown above, add tasks, and color-code them using Trello's labels (important, not important, urgent, and not urgent—a.k.a. Eisenhower's matrix).

---

[11]http://lifehacker.com/tag/trello

Drag the task cards around to prioritize them and cluster similar tasks together.

It's a neat system for getting the big picture while also focusing on what needs to be done on a day-to-day basis."

Try Trello for free here[12]

- Trello has desktop and mobile compatibility.

- Chrome Extension available

---

[12]http://www.trello.com

ASANA

Trello not your cup of tea?

Asana is a project management system as well.

You can drill down on tasks for those of you who would like things to be as specific as possible.

The process of building out projects in Asana is not as visual as Trello, but once you learn the platform it can be very useful for you and your team if you don't mind the lack of visuals.

Try Asana here[13]

- Asana has desktop and mobile compatibility.

- Chrome Extension available

---

[13]http://www.asana.com

HABITICA

If you like games and productivity, you will love Habitica. It is an application that is completely open source (which means anyone can contribute to making it better) and is designed like old school RPG's (role playing games).

You get to create a character that you can customize with various items like helmets, shields, and magic items.

As you complete tasks to your to-do list, you gain "experience points", gold coins with which to purchase new equipment, and can even unlock digital pets like lions, tigers, bears and dragons (oh my!).

Habitica even has fun sound effects and a community of people just like you who are working at improving their daily lives through goal setting and overcoming distractions.

You can also team up with friends or co-workers to take on large projects together in a fun way.

Ryan taught himself how to play the piano by setting up daily reminders in Habitica to play regularly.

The app has been featured in various large publications and is used by people all over the world.

Game on!

Sign up for Habitica for free here[14]

- Habitica has desktop and mobile compability.

---

[14]http://www.habitica.com

LUMEN TRAILS

The founder of Lumen Trails designed the app to help himself quit smoking cigarettes.

It has since evolved into a massive number of templates and resources to help its users track and sort through all kinds of data.

Ryan uses Lumen Trails to track everything from time spent working on client projects for his creative agency to his car mileage.

It can also be used to track progress for things like working out, sleep patterns, weight loss programs, etc.

We even know someone who used a customized template in Lumen Trails to wean down off of a very addictive anti-depressant medication.

The uses are only limited by your imagination.

Below is the text from their website at the time of this writing:

"Give your busy mind a break. With this app, you will never forget anything again. Lumen Trails lets you take notes, make lists or keep track of other things in your life, such as time, workouts, expenses, calories, food, weight, sleep or anything else you can think of, even where you've parked your car.

The beauty of Lumen Trails is that you can track anything. There are tons of other apps that allow you to track one or two things, for example, calories and weight. But what if you decide to track something else? Say, how many cigarettes you smoke as you try to quit, your eating habits or even net worth? Lumen Trails is the app for that!

Instead of having one app for your to-do lists, one for tracking expenses, another one for tracking your weight, you can declutter your home screen and just have one app that does it all.

So what's truly important to you right now? Your Health? Fitness? Finances? Productivity?

Track it and get things done."

You can download Lumen Trails on the Apple App Store or visit their website at LumenTrails.com

- Lumen Trails is, at the time of this writing, only available on iOS/Apple devices

TICKTICK

For more of a checklist/to-do list type of tool we recommend TickTick.com.

We really like the checklist functionality of TickTick, but we wouldn't necessarily recommend it for project management.

We were using TickTick before we moved over to Trello.

Here is a great review of TickTick from Life Hacker with an excerpt below.[15]

> "Adding new to-dos is as easy as typing them, and you can set deadlines and set custom reminders for specific times of day.
>
> You can set the to-do to recur every day, week, month, or year, complete with specific repeat days, so you can have a daily to-do repeat every five days, for example.
>
> You can even set when the to-do should stop recurring. Like any good to-do app, you can organize your items into lists to keep them separate, and get a daily or weekly view of everything you have coming up.
>
> You can add notes to individual to-dos, create lists with to-dos and subtasks beneath them, and share to-dos with other users."

Try TickTick here[16].

-TickTick has desktop and mobile compatibility.

- Chrome Extension available

---

[15]http://bit.ly/1mwXgWi

[16]http://www.ticktick.com

Automating Your Digital Life

Are you pulling your hair out trying to manage and maintain your presence on Facebook, Twitter, your website, Tumblr, Instagram, Google+, and everything else?

Would you like to know the secret to getting a handle on all of this stuff?

We believe it is all about learning how to automate as much as possible so that the systems you build work in the background of your business and your life without requiring that you think about or micromanage them.

Automation is your life preserver when it comes to managing your online presence.

It can also make you feel like you're drowning if you don't do it properly!

One of the best ways to automate your processes is to find tools that allow you to use a scheduling feature for all your posts.

If a tool does not have a scheduling feature, we would approach it with caution.

Next are the tools that we recommend for automation and how we use them on a regular basis.

Just a heads up - you can use a few of these automation tools in conjunction with each other.

You can set up each tool individually as well as set them up to pull and push content from your different social media platforms.

Everyone will have a different strategy to implement with automation and after you go through these options you can define what your personal strategy will be.

Keep in mind that with automation, this will take a *lot* of trial and error on your part to figure out exactly the processes that will work for your specific needs.

You've also got to remember that nobody likes feeling 'spammed' with information so just use these things with caution!

99
body## IFTTT

The first automation tool that we use is IFTTT.com.

It stands for "if this, then that", and their tagline is "put the internet to work for you."

This is one of the most powerful tools that we've come across on the internet because it allows you to define your own "recipes" for automation.

There is an active and helpful community that works together to give ideas to each other for how to use the software to their advantage.

Jill Duffy from PCMag.com describes it perfectly:

> "Use IFTTT to create "recipes" of automation—no code or scripting required—and kiss your worries goodbye...It's a free website and service that lets you automate simple tasks in your digital life, such as "if there is an upcoming event on my Google Calendar, then send me a text message reminder with the event name, time, and address..."
>
> Read more here.[17]

As we mentioned, be careful with IFTTT because if you get too carried away with your "recipes" you are going to overload your digital space and no one is going to want to follow you!

(We say this because we've both done it.)

Start with IFTTT as a baseline for automation and then you can move on from there.

---

[17] http://bit.ly/1n366tn

You can create an unlimited number of recipes.

We recommend that you start with 1-3 simple recipes to get an understanding of how it works and then you can build on that foundation.

Try IFTTT here.[18]

- IFTTT has desktop and mobile compatibility.

---

[18]http://ifttt.com

FRIENDS+ME

If you have a Google+ account and want it to be your main social media platform that you post to, this automation tool is one of the only ones we've found that allows you to do so.

There is a free version and also a premium version available. The premium version allows you to post only to Google+ and Friends+Me automatically publishes the content to all of your other social media channels.

This one isn't as user-friendly as we would like, but once you figure out how to use it, it can easily become an indispensable tool in your social media arsenal.

Denise Wakeman of Social Media Examiner has a great review here[19] and shares how to best use this tool.

Here's a quote:

> "...you can manage exactly where you want to re-post your content. Recently, Friends+Me added a scheduling feature that you can choose to enable or disable.
>
> By scheduling reposts, you control the day and time they show up on your other networks.
>
> For example, you may not want your Google+ posts to simultaneously publish to your other social profiles. You can easily schedule them to post to those networks as soon as 5 minutes later or up to 3 days later."

[19]http://bit.ly/1n366tn

One of the other features that we love is the ability to select which social networks you will publish to (or not) with the simple use of custom hashtags.

Try Friends+Me for free here.[20]

- Friends+Me has desktop and mobile compatibility but does not have a mobile app.

---

[20]http://mbsy.co/6rprs

DOSHARE

Another automation tool that is specific to Google+ is DoShare.

DoShare is a Chrome extension that runs in your web browser.

DoShare does not pull any posts from any other platforms or automation tools.

It also only pushes posts to Google+.

DoShare is ideal for scheduling posts into Google+ when you are not available or don't have the normal time to put into your social media.

DoShare's layout is exactly like a Google+ post, so if you are familiar with posting to Google+ you shouldn't have any trouble.

Get DoShare here[21]

- *Chrome Extension available*

---

[21]http://goo.gl/LXQ3wJ

Again, pay attention that you do not flood your digital space.

Be specific in scheduling your posts and make sure that you spread things out accordingly.

Automation is a big piece of the efficiency puzzle for many social media and online/digital business owners, so use it wisely.

There are many more automation tools that you can use and you are certainly free to do a Google search to find others that work for you.

Password Management

Now that we have covered automation, are you looking at all your passwords that you have to keep track of?

It's next to impossible to do that, right?

Well, there are tools for that also!

We would recommend at the very least keeping a little black book of your passwords in a safe but accessible place.

If you're looking for a digital tool for password management, however, LastPass is a good option.

LASTPASS

LastPass is your password vault!

It is an amazing tool that helps you organize and keep all your passwords secure.

You can organize your passwords into different folders.

You can update logins and passwords anytime AND the program lets you know when you have duplicates.

Lifehacker once again brings us a slew of reviews and articles about LastPass.

You can read more about LastPass here.[22]

---

[22]http://lifehacker.com/tag/lastpass

Try LastPass here[23]

- LastPass has desktop and mobile compatibility

- Chrome Extension available

---

[23]http://www.lastpass.com

The Big List

Below is a list of tools that we've mentioned and a few that we haven't, organized by category.

Enjoy!

PROJECT & LIFE MANAGEMENT

Evernote[24]

Dropbox[25]

Trello[26]

Asana[27]

Habitica[28]

Lumen Trails[29]

TickTick[30]

ThriveSolo[31] - Great for freelancers

WorkFlowy[32] - A workflow organizing platform

---

[24]http://goo.gl/xshMLr
[25]http://www.dropbox.com
[26]http://bit.ly/1gnDfRR
[27]http://www.asana.com
[28]http://www.habitica.com
[29]http://www.lumentrails.com
[30]http://www.ticktick.com
[31]http://www.thrivesolo.com
[32]https://workflowy.com

CamCard[33] - A business card reader

AUTOMATION

IFTTT[34]

Zapier[35]

DoShare[36]

Friends+Me[37]

HootSuite[38] - Another social media scheduling software

Buffer[39] - Yet another social media scheduler

---

[34]http://www.ifttt.com
[35]http://www.zapier.com
[36]http://goo.gl/LXQ3wJ
[37]http://mbsy.co/6rprs
[38]http://bit.ly/1ijlCy3
[39]https://bufferapp.com

CRM SOFTWARE

Nimble[40]

Streak[41]

Insightly[42]

Salesforce[43]

BaseCamp[44]

17 Hats[45]

---

[40]http://www.nimble.com

[41]http://www.streak.com

[42]http://www.insightly.com

[43]http://www.salesforce.com

[44]http://www.basecamp.com

[45]http://www.17hats.com

GOOGLE+ TOOLS

Circloscope[46] - Manage your G+ circles with ease!

Hangout Mastery[47] - Learn how to master your G+ Hangouts On Air

---

[46]http://www.circloscope.com
[47]http://www.mastery.thehangouthelper.com/

OTHER STUFF

100 Useful Websites[48] - here's a big list of a lot more useful websites

Bit.Ly[49] - A URL shortener that provides analytics, etc.

Goo.gl[50] - Another useful URL shortener that functions similarly to Bit.ly but is through Google

OneTab[51] - Tired of all those tabs staying open and clogging your internet space?

Slack[52] - This tool is perfect for communication for teams. Incredibly powerful if you take the time to learn how to use it

Typeform[53] - Great for surveys, contact forms, even sales

Wave[54] - Accounting/invoicing software for small businesses - this is a game changer

---

[48]http://goo.gl/DfDgFG
[49]http://bit.ly
[50]http://goo.gl
[51]https://www.one-tab.com/
[52]http://www.slack.com
[53]http://www.typeform.com
[54]http://www.waveapps.com

We hope you benefit greatly from the resources we have compiled here.

If you know of others that you think would be great to share, please contact Ryan on Twitter[55] and let him know!

---

[55] http://www.twitter.com/ReformDesigns

CHAPTER 7 - Final Thoughts

"Only one who devotes himself to a cause with his whole strength and soul can be a true master. For this reason mastery demands all of a person."

— Albert Einstein

Well, this has been fun! We have worked our tails off to get this little slice of Heaven into your hands.

Let us be straight with you.

We're going to tell you a little secret!

When we wrote this book, we were so distracted!

Yes, it's true. We let every distraction get in the way and it took *a lot* longer to get this done than we had planned.

So we can admit it - we are telling on ourselves. It is incredibly easy to get distracted, especially when working on something like your first real book.

We are human too.

We had our Google Hangout chats open and were sending goofy comments and pictures back and forth.

We both had real life issues going on as well that were true distractions.

Ryan and his wife were forced to move out of their living arrangement of four years and needed to find a new place to live and move to a new state because their landlord was moving back into the house they were renting.

They moved their business and their lives from Silicon Valley to Salem, Oregon in a relatively short period of time.

Once there, they had to move AGAIN because they discovered black mold in the baseboards of the apartment they were renting!

While that was going on for Ryan, Lany started helping her aunt take care of her great uncle who had dementia and then her mother who was diagnosed with cancer, had a car accident, then fell down her stairs and broke her foot!

On top of all of that, we consistently found more things that we needed to do before actually releasing the book to the public.

It took over a year after publishing the first edition e-book version of this book until we were ready to publish the paperback!

We won't break down everything that we were distracted by here, but understand that we deal with distractions too.

Just like you, we dealt with our own stuff while we were writing this book and simultaneously running our individual businesses and organizations!

It was challenging to say the least.

So don't tell us that you can't get stuff done!

We decided that we could put this book on the back burner or we could just keep moving forward regardless of the distractions and the time it was inevitably going to take to complete it.

What do you think we did?

Well, if you are reading this now, then the answer should be quite obvious!

We had a *decision* to make - keep moving forward, or just throw in the towel.

Time management is often just something that most people talk about and say they need to do, but NEVER get serious about putting into practice.

Take a look at the choices you make. Be honest with yourself about how you are spending your time.

When you know you've got to do a certain number of things before you'll see the results you desire, spending several hours binging on Netflix isn't going to help you get there faster!

As we said at the beginning and all throughout this book, **time management is a CHOICE.**

Your choices have set you on the course you are currently on today.

You're not living Groundhog Day over and over again, so you have the opportunity to use your experiences to improve your process and strategy.

We have been tweaking and perfecting our processes for a long time. They are never going to be perfect and we will always be making changes.

Have you ever felt like you've been working on something forever and it will never be finished?

Just when you think it's done...something else shows up to slow you down or stop you?

All of your i's are dotted and all of your t's are crossed...or so you think!

Or in our case, you have ordered several proof copies of your book - each time thinking it was done and ready to go - only to find more typos and problems?

Does it ever feel like some force of nature is trying to keep you from publishing that book, creating that product, or taking your business or life to the next level? Steven Pressfield calls it "Resistance". Some people would attribute it to evil forces trying to hold you back from your potential.

Whatever it is and whatever you call it, it happens.

There is no one that we know who doesn't struggle with this issue.

We have worked with successful authors, speakers, coaches, and business owners from around the world - and one of the main things they have in common is that they always encounter resistance in one form (or many) when trying to accomplish a goal they have set for themselves.

No matter how efficient you are, no matter how organized and on point you are...resistance happens.

It can feel like no matter what you do, no matter how hard you try...that everything is conspiring against you to stop you from accomplishing that goal.

Sound familiar?

What the @#%!, right?

(*Yes, we use 4 letter words sometimes when we're frustrated - just like you do...*)

So what to do?

Just breathe.

That's right. In. Out. In. Out.

Oh wait, we need to be doing that exercise too.

Look, we get it. This stuff can be really, really hard sometimes.

MOST times.

It sucks to fight an uphill battle. It sucks to keep making mistakes.

You may find yourself wondering how many times you can hit a brick wall before it comes crashing down on top of you.

You may find yourself wanting to throw in the towel and never look back.

But don't quit.

Whatever you do, don't...F'ing...quit.

It's really all going to be okay, dear reader.

The true test is how you deal with resistance when it happens over and over and over.

Do you realize that we are just as OCD as some of you and we like things to be perfect too?

Do not let perfection get in the way of progress!

This is something that we have to remember and remind ourselves of each and every day.

Keep moving forward. If it takes 10 edits, then it takes 10 edits. Allow the extra time and attention to create a better product or service. Try to look at it like everything is always in development and stages of growth.

Don't beat yourself up about it and recognize that life is a journey, not a destination.

Maybe you need to slow down. Maybe you need to plan better before you take action.

Maybe there is a lesson to be learned somewhere in all of the struggle.

We find that if you take the time to sit back and evaluate your decisions before making them, you can see the big gaping holes in your plan and you can fill them before you fall in.

This is one of our all time favorite topics because it is applicable to each and every one of us in every area of life.

Time mastery is something that we really struggled with and fought against at first, but we pressed on and have learned many valuable lessons that will impact us for the rest of our lives.

This book is not about managing your social media presence even though you can apply the tools and resources in this book for that purpose.

This book is meant to help you manage your time, prioritize

your activities and when that is said and done actually make more money so that you have more freedom!

You have now been equipped to be able to fine tune your big picture.

Take what we've shared and build a strong foundation on your core values and what is important to you.

You have learned how to take actionable steps and been given the tools and resources that will help you manage your businesses, your life and your digital space.

In the time that we have taken to write this book, we have changed many of our own resources and tools.

We are constantly on the lookout for things that will help us fine tune what we do.

In an ever-changing and fast paced economy, self-education is the only real "job security" that we believe in.

Robotics and technology continue to advance at a lightning-fast pace - and with access to the internet, you can pretty much learn anything for free.

Use this to your advantage and learn new skills that you eventually can monetize.

We've been asked to share the information in this book quite often and once we started chatting about it, it made sense to combine our knowledge and share it with all of you.

We wanted to write this specifically from the perspective of those who have learned, failed, made adjustments and tried again.

We're not perfect or famous...yet!

But we were tired of the same old gurus not teaching the HOW-TO's!

It is so infuriating to buy a book, a video or an audio series and receive all this great info and "you can do it!" hype, but never learn the most important thing...HOW TO DO IT!

And that is precisely why we have done our best to provide a "behind the scenes" look into the way we do things and how we are able to remain as productive as we are.

By completing this book, you just gave yourself a huge jump start to creating a new path for yourself and your family.

We are so excited for you!

You will be able to repeat and improve on the work you have just done month to month and year to year.

You are in the midst of developing and creating the methods and processes that will sustain your life and business from now on.

We want to encourage you as you start on this journey to focus on yourself. Focus on the areas that you want to improve.

Don't beat yourself up for what you've done in the past...move forward and learn from those mistakes.

And most importantly, don't beat yourself up for not being where you'd like to be yet just because other people have seemingly "arrived".

"Never compare your beginning to someone else's middle." — Jon Acuff

We are all in different places in our lives and businesses. We cannot compare ourselves to those that have gone before us.

We cannot compare our current journey to the Steve Jobs' and Oprah's of the world.

They all started somewhere.

Stay focused on YOU and YOUR journey and you won't be tempted to get discouraged!

We hope that you've learned a lot as you've worked through this with us.

If you have any questions, please feel free to reach out to us on social media or via our websites and we will do our best to get back to you in a timely manner.

Now stop wasting time and burning money and get out there and create something amazing!

Thanks from Ryan

I would like first of all to thank my wife Laura for the incredible outpouring of support, love, and encouragement she has given me throughout this journey so far. Of anyone I know, she knows me the best and loves me still. There's nothing in the world like that feeling.

To my parents - thank you for always believing in me and encouraging me to pursue my dreams, regardless of how crazy they sound to some people. "I'll be right back, after these messages!"

To my sisters - you both have grown up to become amazing women of strength and joy. I look forward to spending more time together soon.

To Brent & Daniel, thanks for always being there to bounce ideas off of, no matter what time it is or how ridiculous they might seem at first. Thank you for always being great listeners. It means more than you know.

To our dear friends and mentors at the Chemeketa Small Business Development Center - there are few people who have truly been "in our corner" in the practical sense of helping grow our business and our vision for the future like you have. You are wonderful people and the dedication you have to helping small business owners is unmatched.

To Rebecca Clayton & Toni - thank you for who you are and what you do and always reminding me to keep looking forward.

To Gwynn & Marshall - your friendship, humor, understanding and your listening ear has been very appreciated since we moved to Salem. Thank you.

To Kim Leighty & the Salem Chamber of Commerce - thank you for helping us get connected and being a champion of what we do.

In no particular order, I'd also like to thank Brendon Burchard, Tim Ferriss, Josh Kaufmann, Rick & Robbi Frishman, David Hancock, Jack Canfield, Audrey Hagan, Alex Carroll, Pete and Yvi, Simon B, James Altucher, Ki, Carol, Susan, Christy, Steven, Andrew, Jaren, Stacy & Terry, Dennis, Brandon, Jim Kwik, the Buffer team, the Typeform team, the Trello team, Laurie Laizure, Zara Altair, Ravinder Lal & Joe Siecinski.

There are so many others and you know who you are. Thanks to all of you who have believed in and championed us!

Thanks from Lany

To Stephan Hovnanian - Thank you for being my go to person for all my out-of-the-box ideas. You have been a big part of why I do what I do and are an example of the kind of business leader that I look up to.

You have always been there to help me refine my ideas and have always been more than willing to help spread those ideas and see them come to fruition. Your innovative, service-focused approach to leadership is an inspiration to many and I am among them.

To Sheryl Loch - thank you for always keeping me on the straight and narrow path to success and reminding me that even when things are tough that you are in my corner to kick my ass when I need it!

I couldn't have done so much of what I'm doing now without you and your dedication to seeing me overcome the obstacles that life throws our way has been a huge inspiration.

To my parents, I wanted to thank you for always challenging me to go beyond what others thought is possible.

My work ethic and determination to succeed has come directly from things I have learned from you and I cannot thank you enough for it.

...and thank YOU!

Thank you for supporting us and checking out our first book!

What we thought we could accomplish in just a few weeks turned into a couple of years of intense work, planning, prepping, editing, and a whole lot of other things that we never anticipated.

We hope that you have enjoyed this book and that you will share it with others.

Please visit StopWastingTime.Today[56] to help spread the word or find out more information about the book.

Also, please use the hashtag #StopWastingTime when sharing on social media.

We'd love to hear your feedback, address any questions you may have or celebrate your successes with you!

And seriously - if you find typos - please let Ryan know as soon as you find them.

Really.

:)

---

[56]http://stopwastingtime.today

About Ryan J. Rhoades

Ryan has been a writer and a multimedia creator since the mid-1990's. He is the founder & creative director at Reformation Designs, a full service creative agency that he and his wife started in Silicon Valley in 2011.

Apart from the last 20 years of design experience, Ryan is an author, speaker, creative consultant, web designer, EDM & video producer, and most importantly, a husband to his wife Laura. Some of his recent clients include Jack Canfield, Jim Kwik of SuperheroYou and Kwik Learning, Rick Frishman, Morgan James Publishing, and many others. His clients have appeared in Forbes, The New York Times, The Huffington Post, etc. and appeared on various networks like CNN, MSNBC, and Fox.

Ryan & Laura have had the extreme pleasure of reaching and inspiring hundreds of thousands of people with their work and thrive when helping people just like you get your message out to the world. They currently live in Salem, Oregon with their 3 cats and a ball python.

Connect with Ryan:

Visit www.reformationdesigns.com

Social Media: @ReformDesigns

About Lany Sullivan

A multi-talented entrepreneur, business coach and consultant, Lany Sullivan's passion is building, training, and shaping sales teams to achieve the company's goals, both in developing team objectives and inspired marketing.

Lany has spent years in the trenches building successful sales teams, navigating a diverse range of individuals both in managerial and sales roles.

One of the secrets to Lany's success is her focus on time management, increasing efficiency within an organization and improving systems to work for the company, not against it. These are skills she honed while managing the large-scale marketing promotions and sales for multi-national corporations. She zeroes in on the places where processes could be improved to create efficient systems that save time and money.

Connect with Lany:

Visit www.lanysullivan.com

Twitter: @LanySullivan

Google+: +LanySullivan

CHAPTER 1 NOTES

CHAPTER 2 NOTES

CHAPTER 3 NOTES

CHAPTER 9 NOTES

CHAPTER 4 NOTES

CHAPTER 5 NOTES

CHAPTER 6 NOTES

CHAPTER 7 NOTES

ADDITIONAL NOTES

Made in the USA
Coppell, TX
22 February 2022

73930938R10089